Bless

Bless by Tiffany Nesbitt

Published by Streamroots, 63 Via Pico Plaza #201, San Clemente, CA. 92672. STREAMROOTS.COM

Graphic design by Rachel Allene (www.rachelallene.com).

Accompanying videos and other resources available at BlessBibleStudy.com

Printed in the United States of America.

For Freddi Mae and Alice, who laid the foundation.

Access the teaching videos at
Videos.BlessBibleStudy.com

Access leader resources at
Resources.BlessBibleStudy.com

Beloved sister,

Welcome to *Bless!*

What an honor it is have you here, beautiful one.

More than reaching a particular destination, Bless is about the journey. It's a pressing into Jesus and uncovering more glory, more intimacy than we imagined possible.

Because there's *always more* in Him.

You may find this study to be a bit different than others you've encountered. Rather than launching into the teaching sessions during your local gathering, you'll be able to access the videos online, watching them whenever it compliments your schedule. And rather than experiencing daily homework assignments paired with questions to complete, you'll walk through a weekly guided meditation focused on the nuggets tucked into Psalm 103. It's a gentle dance, timed to the music of the Holy Spirit as you move throughout your days.

The scriptures are the meat of our study, and they're meant to be relished. Take the time to open them wide, savoring the sweetness. Our nine weeks together hinge on these passages, because it's only when we embrace a thorough soul-soaking in the Word that genuine transformation takes place.

Along the way you'll come across a *selah* or two. These pauses are breathing spaces crafted just for you. You'll have the opportunity to interact with sisters from around the world as they explore the psalm, sharing their unique thoughts and individual responses. Be sure to set aside a few moments for reflection, embracing fellowship with the Father and allowing Him to lead you further into His heart.

This study is intended to be a smorgasbord for your soul. I pray that as you take your place at the table, you'll drink deeply, relishing the beauty of the Word of God and listening for the voice of the Holy Spirit as He *leads you into all truth* (John 16:13).

Grace and peace,

Tiffany

CONTENTS

To my husband, Chris. Without your encouragement, challenge and sacrifice, this study would never have been birthed. You make my heart soar.

To my children: Jarren, Kylene, Alyssa and Landon. Your kindness and belief sustain me with joy for the journey. I'm crazy about you.

To my family and friends, those who have called out the gold in my life. I am blessed beyond measure to walk with you and daily grateful for your covenantal loyalty.

To my *selah* girls. Your willingness to be risk takers who walk in vulnerability is powerful. I am inspired by you.

To my armor bearers. Your intercession has provided fuel for the fire and strength for the calling. I am humbled by your love.

To Rachel. Your *yes* has proven greater than either of us could have imagined. I am awed by your talent and generous perseverance — thank you.

To Jesus, the author and perfecter of my faith. My love is yours. This is all for You.

bless

Psalm 103

Bless the LORD, O my soul,
and all that is within me,
bless his holy name!
Bless the LORD, O my soul,
and forget not all his benefits,
who forgives all your iniquity,
who heals all your diseases,
who redeems your life from the pit,
who crowns you with steadfast love and mercy,
who satisfies you with good
so that your youth is renewed like the eagle's.
The LORD works righteousness
and justice for all who are oppressed.
He made known his ways to Moses,
his acts to the people of Israel.
The LORD is merciful and gracious,
slow to anger and abounding in steadfast love.
He will not always chide,
nor will he keep his anger forever.
He does not deal with us according to our sins,
nor repay us according to our iniquities.

For as high as the heavens are above the earth,
so great is his steadfast love toward those who fear him;
as far as the east is from the west,
so far does he remove our transgressions from us.
As a father shows compassion to his children,
so the LORD shows compassion to those who fear him.
For he knows our frame;
he remembers that we are dust.
As for man, his days are like grass;
he flourishes like a flower of the field;
for the wind passes over it, and it is gone,
and its place knows it no more.
But the steadfast love of the LORD is from
everlasting to everlasting on those who fear him,
and his righteousness to children's children,
to those who keep his covenant
and remember to do his commandments.
The LORD has established his throne in the heavens,
and his kingdom rules over all.
Bless the LORD, O you his angels,
you mighty ones who do his word,
obeying the voice of his word!
Bless the LORD, all his hosts,
his ministers, who do his will!
Bless the LORD, all his works,
in all places of his dominion.
Bless the LORD, O my soul!

Bless the
Lord oh
my soul

Psalm 103

This sacred bit of time is holy ground, and we're claiming it for a God encounter.

Jesus, pour out a fresh measure of your presence today, even right here in this very moment.

It's time to speak to our souls.

My soul, bless the Lord.

Psalm 34:1-8

"Such is the nature of the human soul that it must have a God, an object of supreme affection."
Noah Webster

The King of all kings blesses us with His abundant, overflowing goodness, and we were created to respond to that goodness in a mutually passionate love relationship. We *barak:* we bow.[1] All that glory, all that lovingkindness poured out, and we bow low to say *it's all you, Jesus. You are worthy of it all and infinitely more.*

So, what keeps us from giving Jesus our whole-hearted, *all-that-is-within-me* blessing?

Tucked into the corners of our hearts, the barbs of unanswered questions and unresolved grief can remain hidden. And as we stir up our souls to cry, *"Bless!"*, they can prick afresh; our praise can become muffled in pain and doubt. To really bless, to really come into our God-given identity of women who unabashedly declare the praises of the Lord, we have to allow the Holy Spirit to oh-so-gently remove those barbs, swathing them in His fragrant ointment of *steadfast love* and *compassion.*

The antidote for our pain is always His good love.

In this declaration of praise, David shares the secret of the *mighty in spirit.* In spite of trials and difficulties, in the midst of fleshly desires which rage contrary to the Spirit, he instructs his soul to move past every deterrent, calling his heart into utter adoration of the King.

Because everything we are, everything we accomplish is to be an act of laid-down love.

And when we speak to our souls, we break the chains of inhibition that enslave us to timidity and self-focus. When we extol the King in spite of heartbreak, we take back territory which was lost due to doubt. When we fix our eyes on His loveliness, something intrinsic shifts within our core. Suddenly, light breaks and joy tumbles forth, transforming.

Job 1:13-22

Jesus, reveal to me those things which hold me back from freely blessing you. Cleanse me in Your love and restore my soul.

Psalm 23

Selah

At last it's clear to me that the way in which my soul blesses the Lord is by thanking Him in detail for all the great things He has done, just as David listed in detail all of God's many wondrous gifts. Lord, may I never cease to bless your holy name by recounting back to You all the marvelous things which you have accomplished. As David has set an example for me, I will exhort myself, always reminding myself to be constantly aware of the importance of praising Your name. May thankfulness be as much a part of me as breathing!

~Pam

reflections

"...and all that is within me, bless His Holy Name!"

Exodus 34:1-8

In **Exodus 33:18,** Moses, his hungry heart fueled by the majesty of God's presence and the holy intimacy he experienced on that mountaintop, makes a bold request.

Show me your glory.

A few verses later, the Lord answers Moses' request for *more of Him*. God passes before Moses in the splendor of His glory cloud, covering Moses with His hand so that he doesn't shrivel from the mere magnitude of God's power.

And as He does, He *"proclaims the name of the Lord"* (Ex. 34:5).

He reminds Moses of who He is.

He is *Yahweh.*

Merciful and gracious.
Slow to anger.
Abounding in steadfast love and faithfulness.
Forgiving iniquity, transgression and sin.

Moses asks for His glory, and the Lord proclaims His name. Because wrapped up in His name is the indescribable truth of who He is, His very essence.

And it's glorious.

Exodus 3:13-15

Malachi 1:11

Philippians 2:5-11

Jesus, Jesus, Jesus
There's just something about that name.
Master, Saviour, Jesus
Like the fragrance after the rain.
Jesus, Jesus, Jesus
Let all heaven and earth proclaim.
Kings and kingdoms will all pass away,
But there's something about that name.[2]

John 20:30-31

Revelation 19:11-16

When we allow our hearts to feast on His name, a holy tremor takes place. Those places of doubt and insecurity which gnaw at our faith are swallowed in vibrant confidence; every dusky place is eclipsed by glory. Then we can boldly make declarations born of honest knowing: *this is my God.*

El Shaddai, God Almighty
The Bread of Life
Yahweh Tsidkenu, the Lord my righteousness
The Good Shepherd
Yahweh Rapha, the Lord my healer
The Vine
Abba, Daddy
Elohim, God the Creator
The Door
Yahweh Yireh, the Lord my provider
Prince of Peace
El Roi, the God who sees
Everlasting Father
Yahweh Shalom, the Lord my peace
Light of the World
Yahweh Nissi, the Lord my banner
The Bright and Morning Star
The *Alpha* and the *Omega*, the beginning and the end
Wonderful Counselor
Yahweh Raah, the Lord my shepherd
The Way, the Truth, the Life

Selah

Jesus, Lover of my soul.
Your passion runs deep. It overwhelms and I cannot escape. It comforts and I lie down replete. Can I discover Your blazing glory to be enough, embracing the furnace of its mighty consumption and finding myself at last richly satisfied? My soul stretches for beauty but stumbles into mundane sordidness once and again. Today, let me soar free and wild and cling to Your loveliness so tightly that nothing can penetrate this union of love.

~Kristen

reflections

week one video reflections

Videos.BlessBibleStudy.com

and forget not all His benefits

"Bless the Lord, oh my soul, and forget not all his benefits..."

In this holy space, let's consecrate ourselves to the King with hearts eager to remember.

Eager to *bless.*

The word *benefit*, which derives from the Latin root *bene* meaning "good" or "well", is defined by Webster as "an act of kindness".[3]

My soul, remember and call to mind His overwhelming goodness, His great kindness.

James 1:17

"Giving thanks is that: making the canyon of pain into a megaphone to proclaim the ultimate goodness of God when Satan and all the world would sneer at us to recant."
Ann Voskamp

One of the enemy's most fruitful lies is the deception that God is not legitimately good. From man's earliest history, Satan has been using this tactic to rob us of so much which the Father has intended for us to possess. His sinister question to Eve in **Genesis 3:1**, *"Did God actually say, 'You shall not eat of any tree in the garden'?"* is the first part of a one-two punch. He quickly follows with *"You will not surely die. For God knows that when you eat of it, your eyes will be opened, and you will be like God, knowing good and evil."*

God's purposefully keeping something from you, foolish girl. Something wonderful.

Eve falls hard for his masterful bit of twisted rhetoric.

Those niggling doubts, those blatant, bald-faced falsehoods that God can't possibly be true-to-the-core good because if He is, *then what about...*

Every one of those devious questions is posed with a singular aim: to destroy true intimacy with our Father.

And the antidote?

By the power of Holy Spirit-breathed faith, we make declarations of *truth.*

Psalm 84:11-12

In the years of promises yet unfulfilled, His goodness is our eternal yes and amen.
In the pain of hopelessness, His goodness is joy poured over our barren places.
In the darkness of grief, His goodness is our comfort, bearing our deepest sorrows.
And in the wreck of brokenness, His goodness is the gentle healer of our souls.

Psalm 31:19

"Why should the wonders He hath wrought
Be lost in silence and forgot?"
Isaac Watts

Psalm 77

Recollection of His benefits is fuel for praise.

reflections

"And forget not..."

Ah! I do forget and so very fast. This lapse of memory has been referred to as "soul amnesia"[4], and I'm inclined to agree.

Forget not... God pardons.
Forget not... God heals.
Forget not... God redeems.
Forget not... God crowns.
Forget not... God fills.

I forget — forget it all in a flash. I allow the Son to be eclipsed by self and circumstance. And in that loss of True Light? Shadows loom; they loom larger than life.

Ah, but in remembering? Hope buds, swells, blooms... no more a starved seedling struggling in shadows but a flower thriving in the sun. As we turn towards the Son, basking in the beauty of His glorious Light touching our lives, we release a fragrance, an incense of praise rising to Him.

Forget not... God pardons all my mess.
Forget not... God heals all my hurt places.
Forget not... God redeems my very beating, breathing life from the shadows.
Forget not... God crowns me, even me, with faithfulness, and compassion.
Forget not... God fills my days to the brim with beauty.

We tell of Him, His story giving life to ours, and He is blessed.

~Rosanna

"...who forgives all your iniquity..."

Isaiah 43:25

He is the One who blots out our transgressions.

An old-fashioned term, *blot.* For some, it can conjure an image of parchment-style paper coupled with inkwell and pen. Smudged puddles cover letters which an author intends to be stricken from the page.

Too often we view ourselves in kind: all marred by inky blotches, our vain attempts to cover the blemish of sin.

But the heart of our Father observes us through a different lens.

Isaiah 1:18

John 1:29

Our sins and transgressions, though scarlet in intensity, are covered with the blood of the Lamb. A divine exchange takes place — propitiation — and the spot is not left doubly darkened but completely, miraculously clear.

2 Corinthians 5:21

And what of sin's bedfellows, guilt and condemnation?

Psalm 32:5

Psalm 51

"I need not walk through the earth fearful of every shadow, and afraid of every man I meet, for sin is washed away; my spirit is no more guilty; it is pure, it is holy. The frown of God no longer resteth upon me; but my Father smiles, I see his eyes, — they are glancing love: I hear his voice, — it is full of sweetness. I am forgiven, I am forgiven, I am forgiven!"
Charles Spurgeon

Is there any rebellion of heart, Lord, which you cannot cleanse, any choice towards self which you cannot purge? Jesus, may I be convicted today of sin so that I might rejoice all the more in your complete, incomparable forgiveness.

"...who heals all your diseases..."

Mark 2:1-11

In Mark's gospel, Jesus makes a claim which astonishes the religious rulers of His time: just as the Son of Man has the power to heal, so does he have the authority to forgive sins.

But the converse is a statement which can astonish, even today.

Just as Jesus Christ has the authority to forgive sins, so does He have the power to heal.

James 5:13-18

As in David's previous assertion "*...who forgives all your iniquities...*", the Psalmist employs one of his favorite adjectives in his next declaration "*...who heals all your diseases...*".

All.

His statement is tied to an unspoken question which can't be ignored: is there any sin which God has not the power to forgive?

"But that you may know that the Son of Man has the power on earth to forgive sins..."

Likewise, then: is there any disease which Jesus has not the power to heal?

"'I say to you, rise, pick up your bed, and go home.' And he rose and immediately picked up his bed and went out before them all..."

"Sickness is to our body what sin is to our soul. The same atoning work of Jesus dealt with both."
Bill Johnson

Matthew 4:23-24

Exodus 15:26

May we go out as carriers of His bold and extravagant love, pouring His healing power over our neighborhoods, our cities, our nations. Because *the healing of the nations* is the very heartbeat of our Savior.

Heal us, Father, Yahweh Rapha. Restore our bodies to abundant health through Your almighty power. Mend us completely: body, soul and spirit.

Do I truly believe? To what extent do I trust the Lord of the Universe?

How can I accept His seeming silence when I petition for healing?

I have prayed fervently alongside others for miracles. I have claimed Kingdom promises for my own family. I have whispered desperate pleas to my Papa God for myself.

Do I do so with complete faith for Him to respond? Or am I hindering His desire to bless me with His very best simply because I plead in an attitude of bereavement — perhaps clinging to a partial, hidden expectation that my prayer will not be answered?

The Message translation presents verse 4 of Psalm 103 in these words:

He crowns you with love and mercy — a paradise crown.
He wraps you in goodness — beauty eternal.
He renews your youth — you're always young in his presence.

I am always young in His presence!

The eagle glides effortlessly upon the updrafts, higher and higher into the upper atmosphere, closer and closer to the throne of God. We can obtain this communion with our Father only by opening wide our wings of worship to embrace the presence of the Holy Spirit as we enter into His holy presence.

I have often experienced healing during a worship service. It's happened when I've abandoned myself fully to the Father, immersed myself completely in worship. How incredible it is to abandon all physical pain and worship the Lord without expectation of what may happen next: freedom from pain as I am enveloped within our Father's presence, confidence to ask and freely receive with expectation of His healing as I'm lifted up into the stratosphere of His presence! It's there that I truly trust Him, and I wait with joyous expectation.

~Megan

week two video reflections

Videos.BlessBibleStudy.com

Who
you with
Steadfast
love + mercy

"...who redeems your life from the pit..."

Redeemer of our souls, we bow and bless. Worthy are You, King of the universe.

Those of us who have known trouble can easily relate to the pit. Imprisoned in that narrow cavity which was barren of life and any viable escape options, we were bound in darkness.

Seemingly abandoned.

Genesis 37:1-18

At times, the heartless, self-focused choices of others have flung us into the pit. And sometimes, it's our own stubborn willfulness. But no matter the form of bondage, we were trapped and desperately in need of deliverance.

David reminds the children of God of the eternal character of our Father, prompting us to *remember,* and in all our remembering, to feast on His great *redemption.*

Because the fact is, too often we're selling ourselves short or allowing the enemy to rob us of our inheritance. And no matter how we get there, we can feel beaten up and broken, so deeply in debt that there's no way to repay.

Carted off with a mouthful of grit and no hope in sight.

Lamentations 3:58

Webster defines *redeem* as "To purchase back; to ransom; to liberate or rescue from captivity or bondage."[5]

So Jesus paid the price and we go *free.*

Psalm 40

"Saving us is the greatest and most concrete demonstration of God's love, the definitive display of His grace throughout time and eternity."
David Jeremiah

Psalm 107:1-22

Let the redeemed of the Lord say so.

It's who we are.

Beautifully free with heads thrown back in laughter. Courageously bold, fearless in obedience. Dancing in intimacy with the Lover of our souls. Clothed with strength and dignity, armed with truth. Powerfully walking in the overflow of love.

Redeemed.

Beloved, how can we restrain that song of joyful deliverance streaming from our hearts?

reflections

Selah

"LIGHT," He commanded, and then it was so.
The heavens took form as the earth did below.

"LOVE," He imagined, took from dust to create,
But made in His image, His likeness, His shape.

"JOY!" He exclaimed, creation complete.
In the cool of the night, man and God, they would meet.

Sin was the chasm and pride our despair:
Its violence stripping us naked and bare.

Shame we exchanged for truth and communion.
The love of a Father replaced, disillusioned.

Lost into darkness, we ran to forget.
Hopelessness driving our fear and regret.

Silence stretched over the worn generations,
Making a way for the Savior of nations.

Stirring began from the heavens to the ground,
From the east to the west came the triumph of sound:

"MINE!" He declared. "IT IS DONE IN MY NAME."
"WHAT THE ENEMY STOLE, MY SON WILL RECLAIM."

Died. In our place. He took what was ours.
In His blood our transgressions were turned into scars.

Victory won, chains broken and smashed:
Our Savior redeemed every sin that has passed.

GRACE for our lives to fill and to lift,
For our eyes it must raise, and our hearts it must shift.

"NEW," He reveals. "HOPE WILL NOW SET THE WAY."
"I WILL NEVER FORSAKE YOU OR LEAD YOU ASTRAY."

For as high and as wide as creation attains,
The steadfast love of the Lord shall remain.

~Noel

"...who crowns you with steadfast love and mercy..."

Isaiah 61:1-3

It's the ultimate Cinderella story: that neglected, destitute woman who is unexpectedly lifted from the ash heap and crowned to rule with the King. For don't we know that every right narrative has woven within it the glory of the gospel — glimpses of beauty and goodness which stir an inexplicable thrill in the depths of our souls?

And the glory of our own unique story is found *right here*: we've been crowned with the ***hesed*** of the Lord God Almighty.[6]

Isaiah 62:1-5

In place of filigreed gold, we're offered undeserved mercy. Instead of shimmering gems, we're bestowed with covenantal loyalty.

Steadfast love.

It's the kind of fairytale-ending which every woman's heart craves, soul-hungry for intimacy. A love that doesn't fade to bitter through the years. A love that doesn't turn ugly or walk away cold. A love that engages, cherishes and protects.

I Corinthians 13:4-7

I John 4:7-21

His glorious love crowns us, raising us from the degradation of slavery to the honor of intimate friendship.

John 15:12-17

Psalm 136:1

"He who crowned the heavens with stars was Himself crowned with thorns."
Thomas Watson

Beloved, the crown which we wear is the crown of the covenant. His declaration of covenantal love — sealed with His blood and demonstrated by the crown of shame which He so willingly bore — that declaration is given as payment for our glorious headdress of *hesed*: His breathtaking, never-ending, steadfast love.

reflections

"...who satisfies you with good so that your youth is renewed like the eagle's."

What truly satisfies me?

"Satisfaction! A rare word! It rings like a silver bell... it is a spiritual blessing, a divine grace that comes from the great, satisfying God — the God who is, himself all-sufficient, is the only One who can be sufficient to fill the heart of man. Satisfaction! Why, that means enough, and enough is a feast!"
Charles Spurgeon

What is it that runs to my aching core, permeating it so completely that the hollow emptiness is filled?

Isaiah 55:1-3

Solomon must have been taught well by his father, because he understood that troubling sense of lack which can haunt us. Demonstrated in fallen creation just groaning to be redeemed, lack can cry so much louder than praise. *"The leech has two daughters: 'Give, give,' they cry..." (Proverbs 30:15).* And so often, don't our hearts do the same? Sucking the very lifeblood from the sustenance we've been so mercifully given and then crying how there's never enough.

Not enough strength to fuel my day or cash to fill my wallet. Not enough grace to restore my soul.

Both Solomon and David shared our human vulnerability, our longings. But David in his discernment offers a recipe for renewed youth, the likes of which even Hollywood in all its glitter can't boast.

Push into the Lord, deep into His goodness. Recount His blessings with an overflow of gratitude.

Because the further we press into His heart, the more satisfied we become.

Lack can't live in His presence.

He is the God who satisfies.

Psalm 90:14

John 1:16

Suddenly, those lines of discontent which so easily indent our souls, the striving and concern of the world, begin to fade.

Turn your eyes upon Jesus
Look full in His wonderful face.
And the things of earth will grow strangely dim
In the light of His glory and grace.[7]

John 7:37

Isaiah 40:25-31

All that made-new freshness, that overflow of abundant goodness… it's found right there in Him.

Selah

Among salvation, redemption, healing, and forgiveness, one of the blessings from the Lord we can count on is that He "satisfies [us] with good." Just as we trust that our diseases will be eradicated and our sins absolved, we can have faith that life with the Lord brings us satisfaction that we could never otherwise find.

Life in the world is full of things that can make us happy for a while, but is there anything out there that truly sustains satisfaction? How often do the 'good things' in our lives become burdensome or turn into idols? Pure satisfaction, true completion, only comes from God. He meets our needs, He ministers to our hearts, He answers our deepest desire for love and acceptance. He satisfies our souls as completely as Jesus' sacrifice satisfied our debt. From that place of safety and fulfillment, blessings are exponentially sweeter and even turn the "bad things" we encounter into opportunities for growth and ultimately, joy.

~Ryann

week three video reflections

Videos.BlessBibleStudy.com

The Lord
works
righteousness
and justice
for all

"The Lord works righteousness and justice for all who are oppressed."

Psalm 33:1-5

Psalm 89:14

Even now, Almighty God, bring us before the foundation of Your throne so that we might feast on your righteousness, worshiping at Your feet.

David seems to delight in extolling the character of God at every turn, both in his personal recollection of the Father's goodness and his corporate declaration of the Lord's faithfulness to Israel.

The Lord our God is a worker of righteousness.

This warrior king who faced Israel's enemies head-on grasped the truth that God is eternally active in demonstrating His righteousness.

When the foundations crumble due to the eroding work of evil, when all around is tainted by wrongdoing and right is trampled, *He is at work.*

Malachi 4:1-3

But His righteousness extends beyond His deeds alone. Righteousness is the very fabric of His nature.

He is the origin of all that is true, every spring of virtue finding its source in Him.

Isaiah 51:4-8

We tremble under your mighty hand, O Lord. You are great and awesome, and your deeds are marvelous to behold. Teach us to view ourselves aright in the light of your great righteousness.

Isaiah 64:6

Jeremiah 23:5-6

Yahweh Tsidkenu: the Lord, our righteousness.

It's the divine exchange — our rags for His righteousness. And what's more, the born-again children of God become what no ancient prophet could have invented or even fully envisioned. The Savior hung on a tree of shame so that we might become the righteousness of God.

"Christ took our sins and the sins of the whole world as well as the Father's wrath on his shoulders, and he has drowned them both in himself so that we are thereby reconciled to God and become completely righteous."
Martin Luther

2 Corinthians 5:17-21

And as if that incredible transaction wasn't enough, our Savior delights in bringing justice.

Psalm 9:7-10

Luke 18:1-8

Hasn't He always prioritized the immigrant, the refugee and the wanderer? Don't the scriptures overflow with accounts of His heart burning for the outcast and downtrodden?

Father, may we extend hope to the needy as we walk as ambassadors of your righteous justice.

reflections

Selah

I am not God's lawyer.

There have been many times in my life when people have wanted to engage me in a spiritual battle. I don't mean a "forces of evil in the heavenly places" type of spiritual battle, but more of a "courtroom drama" spiritual battle. They desire to be the prosecuting attorney and I, of course, am expected to be council for the defense.

Who is on trial? Jesus!

We both have our expert witnesses — they have atheists and scientists with their worldly logic, and I have a Bible and the personal testimony of a woman who once was lost but now is found. Their Exhibit A is a photograph of a suffering child in Sudan, a child who appears to be forgotten and abandoned. My Exhibit A is both the indictment of I John 5:19: ***"We know that we are of God, and the whole world lies under the sway of the wicked one,"*** *and the promise of Psalm 37:10:* ***"Just a little while longer, and the wicked will be no more; You will look at where they were, and they will not be there."***

Although everything I've stated throughout the trial is true, can I prove it undeniably? Sadly, no. I can't prove truth to someone whose eyes are blind because they choose to believe the lies of the enemy. I can't prove truth to someone who ***"lies under the sway of the wicked one."*** *In the end, it's a hung jury, and I pray for another opportunity to present the testimony of the truth of the Word.*

Thankfully, I am not God's lawyer. He doesn't need one. He is the holy and righteous judge and is more than able to represent Himself. However, I **do** *want to be one of His expert witnesses. I have been given a powerful testimony of His enduring love, forgiveness and sovereignty.*

Oh, Lord, choose me to testify! I will sing of Your love forever! The Lord has done great things for me and I am filled with joy!

~Traci

"He made known His ways to Moses, his acts to the people of Israel: The Lord is merciful and gracious, slow to anger and abounding in steadfast love."

God has a history with His people, a story of wooing and redemption. But better yet, it's a narrative in which there are never enough adjectives to describe the protagonist. The hero just keeps showing off a laundry list of jaw-dropping qualities, leaving those around Him awestruck.

One of the key chapters in this tale is the rescue of God's people from Egyptian slavery and their deliverance into the Promised Land. The hero swoops in and with one breath, the seas are parted; the children of Israel travel that watery hallway into freedom and begin their desert wandering. Bread appears in the dust each morning; water gushes from a wall of rock. But as they're traveling, crucial character development is taking place.

They're getting to know their Father.

Who are you really, God?

And isn't that the cry of every searching heart?

Romans 1:19-20

Right from its foundation, His response has been engraved throughout creation.

The spinning of the Milky Way.

The dancing of the aspens.

The pounding of the tides.

"The earth, the surrounding skies — the very mystery and miracle of life itself — all bear witness to a Creator so unlimited in His abilities that men, regardless of their cultural or religious background, have no excuse to not honor Him. Our world is a kaleidoscope of wonders and divinely engineered realities, fitly joined together to showcase the greatness of God."
Francis Frangipane

Psalm 19:1-6

"What is man, that you are mindful of him, and the son of man, that you visit him? (Psalm 8:4)"

Isaiah 65:1-2

We serve a God who longs to make Himself known. He communed with Adam in the cool of the garden. He appeared to the patriarchs, calling them out of ignorance and into covenant. He wooed rebellious Israel to Himself. And because that wasn't enough to restore true intimacy, He stepped into skin so that we might know Him, just as we are fully known.

And even more astounding, He names us *His beloved, His bride.*

reflections

week four video reflections

Videos.BlessBibleStudy.com

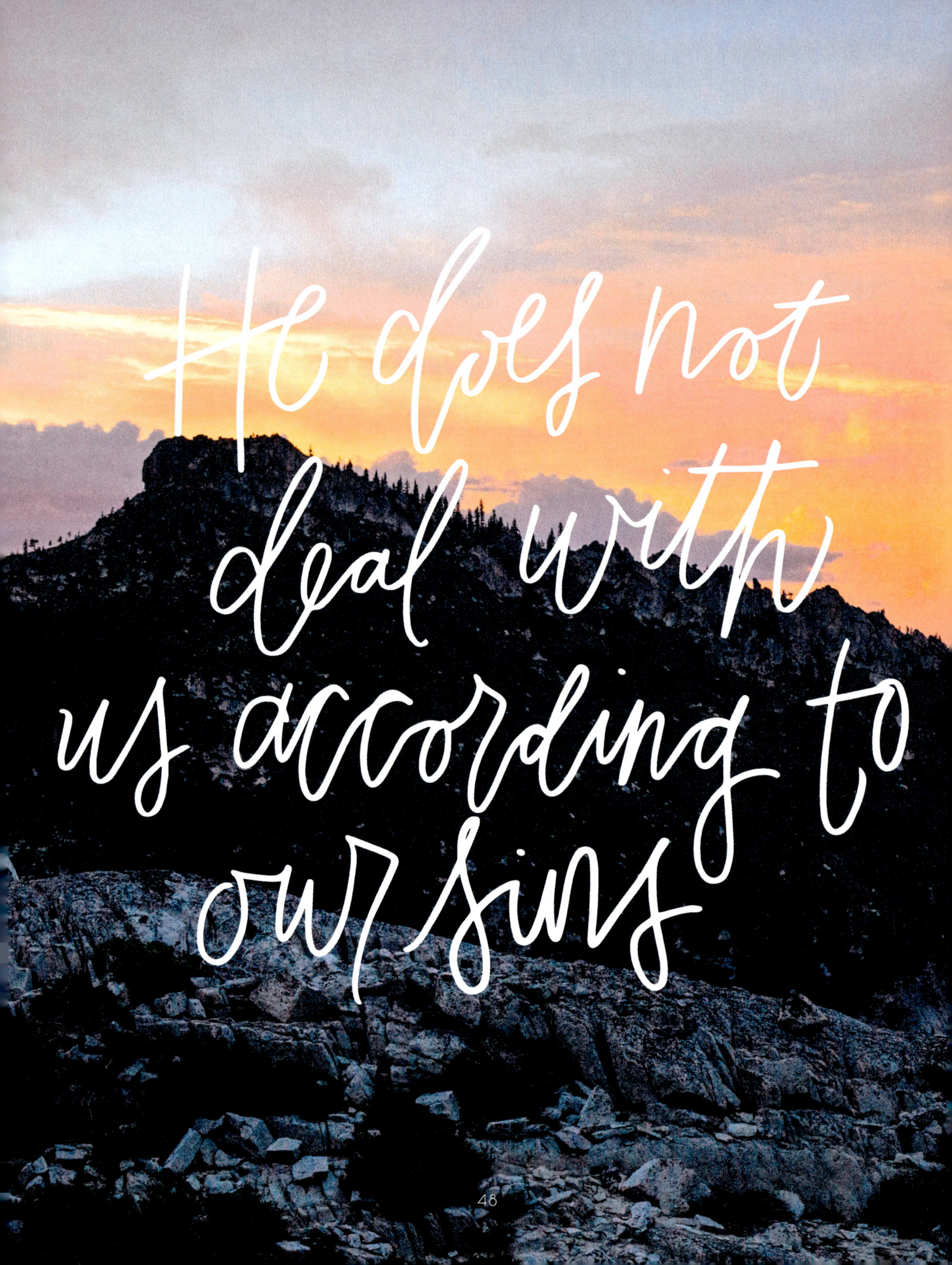
He does not
deal with
us according to
our sins

Week 5

"He will not always chide, nor will he keep His anger forever. He does not deal with us according to our sins, nor repay us according to our iniquities."

As we come into the presence of the Father, may we quiet our hearts, having ears to hear the whispers of the Spirit.

Jesus, speak to us of Your great love.

Before we clung to the cross for salvation, if we were to stack our sins for an accounting, they would stretch as high as the heavens.

Innumerable.

And if God were like a man, somewhere in the back of His mind would be this rehearsing of every wrongdoing, every offense. Like us, He would have thick walls surrounding His heart because of the rebellious, hurtful choices we've made against Him.

But through inspiration of the Spirit, David teaches that God is nothing like man, for "*He does not deal with us according to our sins, nor repay us according to our iniquities.*"

Instead, He lavishes us.

Ephesians 1:3-23

He has ***blessed us with every spiritual blessing.***
We are ***blessed in the Beloved.***

"Define yourself radically as one beloved by God. This is the true self. Every other identity is illusion."
Brennan Manning

As beneficiaries of the new covenant, we're not treated as we deserve. We stand transformed, complete in the restoration of all that God originally planned to give us, all that He designed us to be.

Romans 8:12-17

Instead of viewing us through the lens of our past, He declares over us a redeemed future. And in the power of that declaration is *everything* we so desperately need but so often miss — already ours because of the extravagant *hesed* of our Savior.

Holy
Blameless
Chosen
Adopted
Redeemed
Forgiven
Lavished

Beloved, it's time for an identity shift.

No more self-deception or wallowing in the lies of self-pity.

The King of Glory has called us by a new name, and that identity has *not one thing* to do with our performance but *everything* to do with His sacrifice. Amazingly enough, we get to choose. We can cling to the decrepit rags of our past, stubborn in our insistence that the old titles still fit.

Or we can walk free.

Deuteronomy 7:6

I Peter 2:9-10

Colossians 3:12-17

Jesus, let us hold tight to this truth, undone by its glory.

Let's unpack the treasures of **Ephesians 1:3-23.** Once we've truly caught hold of these truths, our identities will no longer be bound to the lies of the enemy. Describe with fresh eyes that rebirthed woman, viewing yourself through a transformed Kingdom perspective.

Selah

Who would I be if I were fully me? If I were completely alive to every nuance of the physical and spiritual DNA the Father conceived just to craft me?

What if the layers of self, of sin, of this weary world were peeled back, exposing the raw regeneration of reborn life in Christ?

No more shame to hide behind like so many leaves stripped from nearby foliage, covering my nakedness. No more fear to keep me cowering from intimacy with the One who gave me life. No more hopelessness strangling my joy. No more empty weariness, the residue of endless lies I've embraced.

No more hesitation. No more second-guessing. No more small or tight or not enough. No more what-if's or I-should-have's. No more falling short or reaching too far. No more too-foolish dreams or unfulfilled destinies.

In being fully me, I would be fully alive. I would dance and spin and wonder in the breath-taking awe of new birth, and I would not hold back, not even once. I would stand, fully confident that there is nothing but confidence to be had. I would radiate joy because joy is my inheritance.

What would she look like, that woman I was born to be?

reflections

week five video reflections

Videos.BlessBibleStudy.com

great is
His
steadfast
love

"For as high as the heavens are above the earth, so great is his steadfast love toward those who fear him..."

Let's lay aside the entanglements which catch hold of our hearts and move intentionally into the Lord's fathomless grace.

Come, Lord Jesus.

Our God is a God of covenant.

Adam
Noah
Abraham
Moses
David

Throughout the ages, the Lord has demonstrated His covenantal loyalty to those who would have hearts to receive His affection.

Isaiah 54:10

It was God's steadfast love which bound the hearts of His people into covenant with Him; it was that same steadfast love which kept Him faithful even as all mankind was faithless.

"If we do not believe God cares about us, we will be overly focused on caring for ourselves. If we feel insignificant or ignored by God, we will exhaust ourselves by seeking significance from others. However, once we realize that God truly loves us, that He desires we draw near to Him, a door opens before us into His presence. Here, in the shelter of the Most High, we can find rest and renewed power for our souls."
Francis Frangipane

Isaiah 63:7

"All we like sheep have gone astray;
We have turned — every one — to his own way;
And the Lord has laid upon Him the iniquity of us all."
Isaiah 53:6

Even as we flagrantly flung our sin at Him, He remained loyal. His faithfulness in the face of our faithlessness — it's what makes a way for us to joyfully sing:

"The steadfast love of the Lord never ceases; his mercies never come to an end; they are new every morning; great is your faithfulness."
Lamentations 3:22-23

So we bind ourselves into a love covenant with Him, sealed in the blood of the Lamb. And His *hesed* spills deep over our lives, trickling into crevices and rushing into chasms.

John 15:9

Oh the deep, deep love of Jesus
Spread His praise from shore to shore!
How He loveth, ever loveth,
Changeth never, nevermore!
How He watches o'er His loved ones,
Died to call them all His own;
How for them He intercedeth,
Watcheth o'er them from the throne!

I John 1:5 - 2:6

"...as far as the east is from the west, so far does he remove our transgressions from us."

King David employs two weighty extremes to demonstrate the character of our God.

Heavens above the earth.

East from the west.

Most of us have trained ourselves to ignore hyperbole. We're barraged with it daily in all forms of media, so much so that we frequently tune it out.

But David's use of this technique is not for shock value. Instead, he's intentional in his choice of similes.

In ancient times, astronomers lacked both the tools and the technology to measure the distance between the earth and the limits of the stratosphere. Additionally, the circumnavigation of the globe hadn't yet given the Israelites a comprehension of the earth's vast circumference.

However, as a simple herdsman David had kept watch for hours under the cosmos, studying the expanse of the heavens in his shepherd's vigil. From the blush of dawn to the flame of sunset, he had marked his days by the sun's course.

Psalm 36:5-10

So he employs two boundless extremes to describe the work of God.

He loves us *that* much.

Measureless.

His forgiveness is *that* great.

Without end.

Romans 5:15-17

Romans 8:31-39

Jesus, give us the tongues of angels to sing your never-ending praise, to declare boldly Your steadfast love and forgiveness to those who are caught in darkness, waiting for the revelation of Your light.

"In him is only good,
In me is only ill,
My ill but draws his goodness forth,
And me he loveth still."
Horatius Bonar

Here is Creator, stooping to creation.
Not because creation is intrinsically worthy
Or contains something He needs,
But rather because His love is so wide,
So all-encompassing
That He desired to express it to those who would receive it.
And thus, man was birthed
From love and for love.
Out of the abundance of the heart the mouth speaks,
And He spoke, and it was good
Because He is good.
This truth He proclaimed over mankind, over us,
Binding us to Him in a covenant;
That despite our sin, it is still good.
Because He is good.

~Alyssa

week six video reflections

Videos.BlessBibleStudy.com

the Lord shows
compassion
to those
who fear Him

"As a father shows compassion to his children, so the Lord shows compassion to those who fear him."

Let's offer a sacrifice of joyful thanksgiving, dancing into His courts with hearts eager to praise.

Abba, may we understand the depth of your tenderness for us, walking in reverence before you even as we climb into Your gentle embrace.

Galatians 4:6-7

Our Father is compassionate.

The Hebrew word ***racham***[8]**,** meaning to *show compassion*, also carries the strong connotation of a merciful, caressing love.

But so often, rather than running into our Father's embrace like the treasured daughters that we are, we settle for scraps. And instead of standing securely in His compassion, we swallow the lie of abandonment.

John 14:18-20

What memories still lurk in the shadows of my past, holding me back from the Father's love?

The enemy of our souls lies and deceives, twists and torments. He assures us by every means possible that God is not a trustworthy father, that His embrace is harsh, even cruel.

But despite those tactics of thievery, our Father remains unchanging: *merciful, compassionate, slow to anger and abounding in lovingkindness.*

He's the perfect parent, and in Him there is only good.

Romans 8:15-17

Isaiah 49:13-16

Jeremiah 29:11-14

Father God, I choose to open my heart in vulnerability before you. Let me see your compassion through eyes of hope. Deliver me from the lies of the enemy which have stolen my confidence in you and caused me to question Your trustworthy character. You have engraved me on the palms of Your hands, Abba. You will never leave me or misuse me, but instead, You have plans to give me a future and a hope in Your love.

Selah

Even in the midst of seasons filled with waiting, trials, loneliness and the temptation to take on the weight of this world, we are crowned with steadfast love and mercy from our gracious, unfathomable God. We can approach His throne with boldness, into the arms of compassionate Majesty and Righteousness, celebrating that He does not deal with us according to our iniquities, but removes our transgressions as far as the east is from the west: there is no condemnation for those who are in Christ.

What an incredible gift.

Bless the Lord, oh my soul.

Bless His Holy Name.

~Heather

reflections

"For He knows our frame;
He remembers that we are dust."

Like every good father, the Lord's compassion towards us is based on an intimate understanding of *our true selves.*

Dear ones, don't we have a tendency to strut and puff, propping ourselves with achievements or possessions? We love to parade like peacocks. Displaying only our best plumage, we're eager for the clucking approval from those around us.

But our Father… He *knows* us.

It's a *down-to-the-core* knowing, one that sweeps right past our poorly crafted facades and straight into our souls. And David declares that instead of harboring condemnation for our artificial dignity, the heart of God overflows with compassion.

Because He remembers.

Genesis 2:5-7

He was there at the beginning, back in the Garden when, hungry-heart motivated, He gathered bits of gravelly dust into His palms and just *breathed.*

And man became ***nephesh***[9]***,*** *a living soul.*

That Hebrew word carries all kinds of ideas, but one of the most crucial is the concept of desires, passion, appetites, and emotions: all the qualities that make us unique individuals. They've been inspired by the Father and God-breathed.

But somehow in this whirling hubbub, selective amnesia kicks in and we forget what God remembers. Because we're intent on all those soul-ish aspects of ourselves, we don't live like we've been **twice-breathed** — *born again.* How easily we can neglect the truth: our greatest fulfillment is to bear the image of the One who saved us.

Romans 8:1-11

"You called, You shouted, and You broke through my deafness. You flashed, You shone, and You dispelled my blindness. You breathed Your fragrance on me; I drew in breath and now I pant for You. I have tasted You, now I hunger and thirst for more. You touched me, and I burned for Your peace."
Saint Augustine

I Corinthians 15:39-49

Solomon's wisdom is offered freely.

"The end of the matter; all has been heard. Fear God and keep his commandments, for this is the whole duty of man."
Ecclesiastes 12:13

Help us, Lord, in light of who You are, to rightly remember that we are but dust in Your marred hands.

Rest (n.):
1. freedom from activity or labor
2. peace of mind or spirit

I wish I could remember what it was like, twenty-something years ago, when I didn't care about being perfect. Back when making mistakes was fully acceptable and even encouraged, when falling wasn't scary because I knew my parents would always pick me up and set me back on my feet.

When did that change?

Thankfully, Jesus has taught me that the only true antidote for striving to be made perfect in my own strength is to abide. Abiding in the heart of the Father brings me genuine rest, because when I rest in the Lord, I'm free from labor. Psalm 55:22 states, "Cast your cares on the Lord and he will sustain you. . ." When I cast my cares, anxieties and all other "labors" onto the shoulders of the Most High, He sustains me and gives me the rest that I need.

I also have peace of mind and spirit. The peace of the Lord transcends all understanding (Philippians 4:7). If I'm constantly straining to keep control of my circumstances, I only hurt myself. Jesus wants to grant me peace of mind and a restful spirit, so sometimes I need to make like Frozen's princess, Elsa, and just "Let it go!"

And when I rest in the Lord, I can remain confident in who He is. He's my good Father and faithful friend, the One who knows me better than I know myself.

It's time for me to practice giving up control and let God take care of the rest.

~Jordan

reflections

week seven video reflections

Videos.BlessBibleStudy.com

His Kingdom rules over all

"But as for man, his days are like grass; he flourishes like a flower of the field; for the wind passes over it, and it is gone, and its place knows it no more."

Jesus, you are eternal God and we worship You.

Give us a heart of wisdom so that we might understand how to live rightly before you in these days which you have given us under the sun.

Don't we all long for permanence?

There's something in the heart of every woman which hungers for that which lasts, that which will endure. And so we pilgrimage, flocking to sites of ancient grandeur — the splendor of Rome, the mystery of Egypt — as if in walking the dust of those decaying civilizations, we might grab hold of a fragment of the eternal.

Isaiah 40:6-8

Scripture makes it clear: man is but a breath. Like the vibrant blossoms which we love to display, our lives bloom, then fade and wither, passing away.

Psalm 144:3-4

David understood the brevity of life. As a warrior, he was seasoned on the battlefield, well used to watching men die: soldiers who flourished in their prime, cut down and blown away without warning.

So he reminds Israel that her days of sojourning are brief — not because he enjoys meditating on the morbid, but indeed, David delights in the juxtaposition: declaring hope by extolling the praises of his God.

Psalm 39:4-6

"We each die daily. Happy those who daily come to life as well."
George MacDonald

The contrast between our numbered footsteps and God's grasp of both time and eternity is a theme recorded by many of the psalmists.

Psalm 78

Asaph, the author of the seventy-eighth psalm, is incredibly mission-minded. Verse 39 gives a snapshot of our temporal nature as well as providing motivation for his song.

"He (the Lord) remembered that they were but flesh, a wind that passes and comes not again."

Time is short.

Asaph's call to action is woven throughout the remainder of the psalm:

Let's tell of the wonders of the Lord to the upcoming generation! May we remind them of our history, the truth of our heritage. Let them consider how quickly their moment of glory will pass. And may they be convinced of the unfailing faithfulness of our God!

Moses also understood this crucial truth.

Psalm 90

The crux of his composition, the point on which it turns, is this:

"So teach us to number our days, that we may gain a heart of wisdom."

Paul echoes Moses' prayer in his letter to the Ephesians.

Ephesians 5:1-21

Because it can seem that our chain of days is endless, Paul sagely reminds us: make the best use of your time.

Father, help us to use the inestimable gift of our days in wisdom, offering each one to You as a melody of praise. Allow us to number our moments with discernment, so that we might leave behind us true permanence: a legacy of faith rooted in a passionate pursual of Your heart.

reflections

"But the steadfast love of the Lord is from everlasting to everlasting on those who fear Him, and His righteousness to children's children to those who keep His covenant and remember to do His commandments."

Oh, the contrast!

We're but a breath, a bit of withered grass...

But God.

His *hesed* is so deep, so rich and vast. And more than that —

It has no end.

It continues from *before* time began until *after* time will cease.

Everlasting.

Psalm 36:5-10

The steadfast love of the Lord never ceases.
His mercies never come to an end!
They are new every morning, new every morning.
Great is Thy faithfulness, O Lord!
Great is Thy faithfulness![10]

And that steadfast love is poured out all over those who fear Him, those who honor Him and who walk faithfully in covenantal loyalty with Jesus.

Even more, not only is that loyalty lavished upon His daughters, but because we chase after intimacy with Him, our future generations are blessed with the overflow.

So whether we're stepping with hope-filled eyes into the prime of our lives, or our memory box overflows with the recollection of the many years — we can make a confident declaration of faith over our children, both biological and spiritual.

He is good and His love never ceases.

Psalm 128

Isaiah 54:1-14

Selah

Like the tide, Your love is untamed.
It beckons and draws, wild in its grace.
Your love destroys all my barriers with such poignant accuracy.
It presses on pain until I am broken, until I am known and I am free.
Like the tide, Your love rushes and roars.
Violent in its affection, Your love breaks down walls which covered hidden doors.
Like the tide, Your love consumes, leaving nothing in its wake.
My heart is quenched but still yearning for the safety of Your love, for its strength.
Filled with vibrancy of color, Your love yields newness every morning.
Grace pounds against the shores of my heart until I am unashamed of my story.
"What is fear?" says the tide to my small, quivering heart.
"There is nothing here but safety and adventures waiting to be embarked upon."
So I will cast aside the hollow where the lies hide and wait, and I will throw myself into the tide.
I will choose to believe that the current of heaven sings the song of Your love.
And to the monstrous creatures who attempt to cut my sails:
I will stand here and sing to the wind and the earth of a Light that is great, a Light that prevails.
I will stand here and wait 'til I feel your breath cover me, making me assured.
And then I will rise, I will walk, I will run towards the tide, towards the song that endures.

~Kylene

"The Lord has established His throne in the heavens, and His kingdom rules over all."

Psalm 145

Jesus had a great deal to say about His Father's Kingdom.

As we reconcile the writings of the Old Testament prophets with the unprecedented descriptions which Jesus used, a potent reality emerges.

Matthew 13:24-52

A handful of seed planted in fertile soil.
A tiny speck of mustard birthing a mighty tree.
An uncovered treasure prompting great joy.
A priceless pearl worth all possessions.
A net spread to gather teeming fish.

It's vast, this King's domain: mighty, powerful and beyond our comprehension. It's also fully present, active and alive.

But more than that, the Kingdom is within us. When we bow and yield — it's then that the Kingdom comes in splendor right in our midst. Because the very notion of our King reigning from His throne leads to an inescapable truth: the Father rules in glorious dominion.

Matthew 9:35-38

"The kingdom of God which is within us consists in our willing whatever God wills, always, in everything, and without reservation; and thus His kingdom comes; for His will is then done as it is in heaven, since we will nothing but what is dictated by His sovereign pleasure."
Francois Fenelon

And when the Kingdom comes, Jesus-glory starts breaking out all over.

Luke 4:14-21

Romans 14:17

Carriers of His Kingdom. Ambassadors authorized to bring the rule of the King.

It's who we are.

week eight video reflections

Videos.BlessBibleStudy.com

bless the
Lord oh
my soul

Week 9

"Bless the Lord, O you His angels, you mighty ones who do His word, obeying the voice of His word! Bless the Lord, all His hosts, His ministers, who do His will! Bless the Lord, all His works, in all places of His dominion. Bless the Lord, O my soul!"

Dear ones, let's not hold back. This is the moment to shout the praise of our God with all that is within us.

Bless!

After all this — this poetry of song crafted through description and delight — David comes full circle, right back to the start.

The dancing thrill of exultation within his heart just can't be silenced.

Psalm 104:1

Bless!

Again and again he stirs up his soul from its slumber, calling forth a deeply personal adoration of the King from the recesses of his heart.

But more than that — he commands all of creation, all of the heavenly hosts and angelic warriors to follow suit.

Psalm 134

"Let others murmur, but do thou bless. Let others bless themselves and their idols, but do thou bless the LORD. Let others use only their tongues, but as for me I will cry, "Bless the Lord, O my soul." And all that is within me, bless his holy name. Many are our faculties, emotions, and capacities, but God has given them all to us, and they ought all to join in chorus to his praise. Half-hearted, ill-conceived, unintelligent praises are not such as we should render to our loving Lord. If the law of justice demanded all our heart and soul and mind for the Creator, much more may the law of gratitude put in a comprehensive claim for the homage of our whole being to the God of grace."
Charles Spurgeon

Psalm 135:19-21

And here's the genuine beauty of it all: when we adore Jesus, His blessing pours right back over us in a waterfall of sweet intimacy. It's then that we begin to realize that this love relationship is entirely mutual, and our hunger for Him deepens. We understand that the full measure of both blessing Him and being blessed come from His presence, straight from His heart.

"To have found God and still to pursue Him is the soul's paradox of love, scorned indeed by the too-easily-satisfied religionist, but justified in happy experience by the children of the burning heart."
A.W. Tozer

So let's live blessed, beloved.

Blessed to seek Him.

Blessed to know Him.

Because when we're choosing to live blessed, we're choosing to be undone by the radical grace of God. All our sin, pride, stubborn rebelliousness — those knotty declarations of hard independence — they unravel in the glory which is His *hesed,* His steadfast love. And when we deeply realize that as His daughters, we have unlimited access to the full measure of His blessing, we become who we were created to be — unstoppable in His love.

Bless the Lord, oh my soul!

week nine video reflections

Videos.BlessBibleStudy.com

Psalm 103

The Message

"O my soul, bless God.
From head to toe, I'll bless his holy name!
O my soul, bless God,
don't forget a single blessing!
He forgives your sins — every one.
He heals your diseases — every one.
He redeems you from hell — saves your life!
He crowns you with love and mercy — a paradise crown.
He wraps you in goodness — beauty eternal.
He renews your youth — you're always young in his presence.
God makes everything come out right;
he puts victims back on their feet.
He showed Moses how he went about his work,
opened up his plans to all Israel.
God is sheer mercy and grace;
not easily angered, he's rich in love.
He doesn't endlessly nag and scold,
nor hold grudges forever.
He doesn't treat us as our sins deserve,
nor pay us back in full for our wrongs.
As high as heaven is over the earth,
so strong is his love to those who fear him.

And as far as sunrise is from sunset,
he has separated us from our sins.
As parents feel for their children,
God feels for those who fear him.
He knows us inside and out,
keeps in mind that we're made of mud.
Men and women don't live very long;
like wildflowers they spring up and blossom,
But a storm snuffs them out just as quickly,
leaving nothing to show they were here.
God's love, though, is ever and always,
eternally present to all who fear him,
Making everything right for them and their children
as they follow his Covenant ways
and remember to do whatever he said.
God has set his throne in heaven;
he rules over us all. He's the King!
So bless God, you angels,
ready and able to fly at his bidding,
quick to hear and do what he says.
Bless God, all you armies of angels,
alert to respond to whatever he wills.
Bless God, all creatures, wherever you are —
everything and everyone made by God.
And you, O my soul, bless God!".

Beloved, it's your turn. Boldly ask the Lord to pour His creativity and insight over your heart, praising Him from your core. Remember who He is, all that He's done for you, and honor Him for His goodness in your life. Then, take up your pen and write your own unique psalm of thanksgiving. Offer it as a love-gift to your King.

Our community of sisters from around the world would be honored to read your selah. Will you consider sharing it online? Your vulnerability will strengthen and encourage many others, bringing our Father glory!
Visit ***Selah.BlessBibleStudy.com*** *to post your selah.*

A Psalm of ____________________

Endnotes

[1] "Strong's Hebrew: 1288. (Barak) -- To Kneel, Bless." Biblehub.Com, 2017, http://biblehub.com/hebrew/1288.htm.

[2] Gaither, Gloria and William J. "There's Something About That Name." Because He Lives. Spring House Music Group, 1998. CD.

[3] "Webster's Dictionary 1828 - Webster's Dictionary 1828 - Benefit." Webster's Dictionary 1828, 2017, http://webstersdictionary1828.com/Dictionary/Benefit.

[4] Ann Voskamp, One Thousand Gifts (Grand Rapids: Zondervan, 2011) 106.

[5] "Webster's Dictionary 1828 - Webster's Dictionary 1828 - Redeem." Webster's Dictionary 1828, 2017, http://webstersdictionary1828.com/Dictionary/Redeem.

[6] "Strong's Hebrew: 2617. (Checed) -- Favour." Biblehub.Com, 2017, http://biblehub.com/hebrew/2617.htm.

[7] Lemmel, Helen. "Turn Your Eyes upon Jesus." HymnTime. www.hymntime.com, 2001. Web. Public Domain.

[8] "Strong's Hebrew: 7355. (Racham) -- To Love, Have Compassion." Biblehub.Com, 2017, http://biblehub.com/hebrew/7355.htm.

[9] "Strong's Hebrew: 5315. (Nephesh) -- A Soul, Living Being, Life, Self, Person, Desire, Passion, Appetite, Emotion." Biblehub.Com, 2017, http://biblehub.com/hebrew/5315.htm.

[10] Marsh, Don. "The Steadfast Love." By Edith McNeil. America's 25 Favorite Praise & Worship Choruses, Vol. 3. Jive, 1996. CD.

Made in United States
Orlando, FL
26 October 2022